Gettysburg

July 1-3, 1863

Curtis Slepian, M.A.

Consultants

Timothy Rasinski, Ph.D.
Kent State University

Lori Oczkus, M.A.
Literacy Consultant

Publishing Credits

Rachelle Cracchiolo, M.S.Ed., *Publisher*
Conni Medina, M.A.Ed., *Managing Editor*
Dona Herweck Rice, *Series Developer*
Emily R. Smith, M.A.Ed., *Content Director*
Stephanie Bernard/Noelle Cristea, M.A.Ed., *Editors*
Robin Erickson, *Senior Graphic Designer*

The TIME logo is a registered trademark of TIME Inc. Used under license.

Image Credits: Cover and p. 1 Bridgeman Images; pp. 2, 14 North Wind Picture Archives; p. 4 MPI/Getty Images; pp. 4 to 5 LOC [LC-DIG-pga-07025]; p. 6 LOC [LC-DIG-cwpb-04019]; p. 9 The Protected Art Archive/Alamy Stock Photo; pp. 10-11 LOC [LC-DIG-pga-03235]; pp. 12-13 LOC [LC-DIG-npcc-02151]; p. 13 (left) MixPix / Alamy Stock Photo, (right) NPC Collectiom / Alamy Stock Photo; p. 15 Joe King/ Alamy Stock Photo; p. 16 Eight Arts Photography/Alamy Stock Photo; p. 17 SSPL/Getty Images; p. 18 Classic Image/Alamy Stock Photo; pp. 22-23 Niday Picture Library/Alamy Stock Photo; p. 24 Granger, NYC; all other images from iStock and/or Shuterstock

For reference, a map has been provided on page 21.

Library of Congress Cataloging-in-Publication Data

Names: Slepian, Curtis, author.
Title: You are there! Gettysburg, July 1-3, 1863 / Curtis Slepian.
Other titles: Gettysburg, July 1-3, 1863
Description: Huntington Beach, CA : Teacher Created Materials, 2017. | Includes index. | Audience: Grades 7-8.
Identifiers: LCCN 2016052268 (print) | LCCN 2016052641 (ebook) | ISBN 9781493839278 (pbk.) | ISBN 9781480757875 (eBook)
Subjects: LCSH: Gettysburg, Battle of, Gettysburg, Pa., 1863--Juvenile literature.
Classification: LCC E475.53 .S58 2017 (print) | LCC E475.53 (ebook) | DDC 973.7/349--dc23
LC record available at https://lccn.loc.gov/2016052268

Teacher Created Materials

5301 Oceanus Drive
Huntington Beach, CA 92649-1030
http://www.tcmpub.com

ISBN 978-1-4938-3927-8

Table of Contents

Invading the North

A bugle wakes you. For a moment in the darkness, you think you're back on the family farm in western Virginia. But instead, you're lying on a thin blanket in a tent outside Cashtown, Pennsylvania, in the early morning of July 1, 1863. About two months ago, you left the farm to join the Confederate army. The cutoff age for serving in the army is 18, and you're only 14, but you lied about your age and maybe the army knows that—but the Confederate army needs soldiers. So now you're trying to help the South win a war.

Your job is drummer—and anything else asked of you—in the Army of Northern Virginia under the command of General Robert E. Lee.

The Children's Armies

About 20 percent of soldiers in the Civil War were younger than the minimum recruiting age of 18. One of the youngest was Johnny Clem, who ran away from home and joined the Michigan **infantry** as a drummer at age 10.

A Long March

The Civil War has been raging for almost two years, with the free states and the slave states fighting over the issue of slavery and state rights. Your brigade of tough Virginians has been marching north since May 3. You've passed through Virginia, Maryland, and now you are in Pennsylvania. The immediate goal is to capture Harrisburg, the state capital. Lee hopes this invasion will **demoralize** the North and force it to surrender. Then the Yankees will leave the South alone. Already, many Northern newspapers and politicians are demanding an immediate end to the war.

THINK LINK

- Why is there a cutoff age for joining the military?
- Why do you think some Northerners were calling for an end to the war?

July 1: First Contact

Your brigade is located north of a small town called Gettysburg. General Henry Heth tells the troops that there may be supplies, especially shoes, in the town. Upon getting closer, the presence of Union soldiers is evident. Nevertheless, Heth makes it clear he still intends to search for the shoes. You learn that General Lee has forbidden any combat with the enemy, so some soldiers think the shoe hunt is just an excuse to start a fight.

You've learned how to bang your drum to call officers to council, to get infantry to march together, to sound retreat, and, as you're doing now, to assemble the soldiers. You are ready; you've already tightly rolled up your belongings in your blanket to carry over your shoulder. A tin water cup hangs from your belt, and a **haversack** for food is on your back, since much of your food comes from **foraging** in towns and the countryside.

Approaching Gettysburg

As your brigade marches toward Gettysburg, you hear that George Meade has been made commander of the Union's Army of the Potomac, but no one knows exactly where his army is. A few hours later, as you approach Gettysburg, you realize that you've found Meade's forces. The area is **teeming** with Union troops!

How the Union and Confederate Armies Break Down		
Unit	Number of Troops	Commanded By
Army	At least 2 corps	General
Corps	Union: 10,000 to 20,000 Confederates: 20,000	Lieutenant general
Division (2–4 in a corps)	6,000 to 8,000	Major general
Brigade (2–3 in a Union division; 3–5 in a Confederate division)	1,200 to 4,000	Brigadier general
Regiment (4–5 in a brigade)	400 to 1,000	Colonel
Company (10 in a regiment)	40 to 100	Captain

STOP! THINK...

At Gettysburg, the Army of the Potomac had about 90,000 troops, and the Army of Northern Virginia had approximately 70,000.

- Which Confederate commander had a higher rank, Major General James Ewell Brown Stuart or Lieutenant General Richard S. Ewell?
- About how many extra divisions would the Army of Northern Virginia have needed to total more troops than the Army of the Potomac?

The Battle Begins

Your brigade marches to the crest of Herr **Ridge**, northwest of Gettysburg. East of Herr Ridge is McPherson Ridge, and beyond that lies Seminary Ridge, both of which are currently held by Union soldiers.

Heth orders an attack on McPherson Ridge, and you excitedly drum the call for your first battle! Nearly 7,500 Confederates advance down the ridge and open fire on the enemy. The Yankee **muskets** blast both ends of your line in fearsome **enfilade**, and you have no choice but to retreat in a blind panic up Herr Ridge.

The Yankees Retreat

Your first clash is harrowing, and it's like nothing you have ever seen. There are bodies falling and men hollering in rage and screeching in agony. The rest of your **cohorts** have finally made it back to Herr Ridge to **recuperate**. As soon as General Lee rides by on his horse, Traveller, everyone jumps to their feet in respect. He **exhorts** the men to keep fighting, and they cheer so loud that you can't help but feel renewed in the resolve to fight.

You join the assault as the troops, yelling like demons, dash across the space between Herr Ridge and McPherson Ridge. The fierce charge sends the Yankees scurrying to Seminary Ridge and then into Gettysburg. In the chase after the Yankees, you observe that some of them are bolting through the streets, some are hiding in yards or cellars, and others are heading for a hill east of town.

Hat's Off to Heth

Confederate General Henry Heth was lucky on July 1. His hat was too big, so a clerk had rolled a dozen sheets of paper and put them into the sweatband to make the hat fit. In battle, a bullet hit him in the head. Without the paper cushioning the blow, the shot would have killed him.

General Lee on Traveller

A Civilian Casualty

Of Gettysburg's 2,400 townspeople, only one was killed during the three days of battle. On July 3, a 20-year-old woman was baking bread in her sister's house when a Confederate bullet struck her.

Facing the Enemy

Your brigade gathers at the top of Seminary Ridge. About three-quarters of a mile east, Union troops are pouring onto Cemetery Hill and Culp's Hill at the north end of Cemetery Ridge and onto two hills, Big Round Top and Little Round Top, south of it. The elevated position of the ridge and hills makes the Union position tough to attack.

Meanwhile, a corporal orders you to help collect the rifles of dead soldiers on the battlefield. In a grisly scene, you lug as many muskets as you can back to camp, where a corporal demonstrates how to load a musket in one minute. It takes you 5 minutes to go through all 10 steps, including pushing the gunpowder and bullet down the barrel with a **ramrod**. You'd sure make a slowpoke musket loader!

Longstreet's Legacy

After the war, Confederate veterans criticized Longstreet. They didn't like his lateness to the battle or his negativity about Lee's strategy at Gettysburg. Southerners were also upset when Longstreet later supported the Republican Party, and led an African American **militia** after the war.

The Great Debate

At twilight, you are standing nearby when Lee summons General James Longstreet, his most trusted officer. You overhear Longstreet try to persuade Lee to move his army south to a position between the Union army and Washington, DC, to wait. With the Confederates in position to march to the Union capital, Longstreet says that the Union army "will be sure to attack us. When they attack, we shall beat them." But Lee adamantly says no and points to Cemetery Ridge. "The enemy is there, and I am going to strike him."

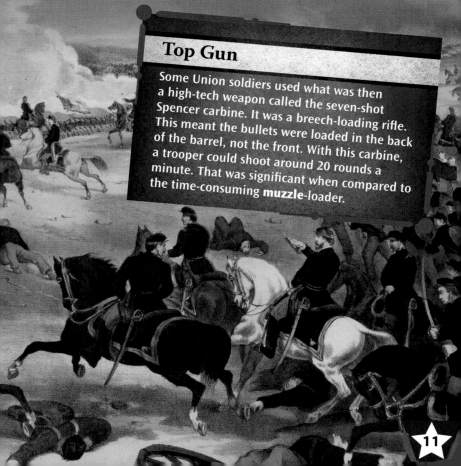

Top Gun

Some Union soldiers used what was then a high-tech weapon called the seven-shot Spencer carbine. It was a breech-loading rifle. This meant the bullets were loaded in the back of the barrel, not the front. With this carbine, a trooper could shoot around 20 rounds a minute. That was significant when compared to the time-consuming **muzzle**-loader.

July 2: Desperate Fighting

On day two of the battle, General Longstreet's division attacks the supposedly lightly guarded south end of the Union position, but things go terribly wrong from the get-go. To begin, Longstreet starts his march two hours late. In an attempt to avoid being seen by the Yanks, he takes his men on a detour, which is an **erroneous** move because it is the wrong road. He then backtracks and takes a route that puts them even farther from where he and his men need to be. When Longstreet finally arrives and takes position, everyone is hot and tired, and even worse—the area is bristling with bluecoats.

Devil's Den

Devil's Deadly Den

The brigade must fight its way past Federals poised a half-mile west of Cemetery Ridge. The Yankees are protecting ground extending south from a peach orchard to a wheat field at the end of a ridge called the Devil's Den. Your fellow soldiers may appear calm, but if they're anything like you, their stomachs are in nervous knots too.

At 4 p.m., the Union soldiers shout, "Here they come!" as your fellow soldiers storm their position at Devil's Den. You end up in a dark area filled with boulders and small caves, where vicious combat takes place. Soon, the Confederates throw the bluecoats out of Devil's Den. You hope the fighting is over, but it's only just beginning.

Honor on the Battlefield

Some battlefield foes respected each other. During one **skirmish**, Confederate Brigadier General John B. Gordon found his Union counterpart, Brigadier General Francis C. Barlow, on the ground badly wounded. Gordon got off his horse, gave Barlow water, carried him to shade under a tree, and agreed to get a message to his wife that he was wounded. Barlow survived, and after the war, he and Gordon became good friends.

Francis C. Barlow

John B. Gordon

Bloody Wheat Field

You hear Confederates whooping and hollering as they join the battle at the wheat field. But the cries are cut short when they're met by blazing guns. The control of the ground shifts back and forth for hours. You sneak close to the action and see a Confederate shot dead as he captures a Union flag, and the Union soldier who grabs it is stabbed with a **bayonet**. You decide it would be wise not to pick up that flag.

As the clash continues here and in the peach orchard, you hear that Confederate General William Barksdale is leading men into the Union line at Cemetery Ridge. It sounds like the Confederates might reach the crest of the ridge, but to your **chagrin**, fresh Union troops force them back, and Barksdale is shot.

Defending the Flag

Soldiers from both sides carried small regimental flags, known as "the colors," which helped troops stay together in battle and find their regiments if they became lost. Some flags displayed the regiment's name, its color, a state seal, the names of battles fought, or inspiring words. Soldiers often died defending their flag or trying to capture the enemy's flag.

A Rough Climb

During the battle, you are swept to the far right of the Confederate line, joining a brigade led by William Oates, who wants to rid Big Round Top of Union sharpshooters. The brigade sprints up the hill, dodging Yank bullets and reaching the peak unharmed. The brigade rests for a moment, but a **courier** orders Oates to take Little Round Top. Now the men scramble down the slope and start to climb Little Round Top, from which they can fire down at the Federals on Cemetery Ridge. Win the hill and the Confederates may win the battle—maybe even the war!

An Officer and a Scholar

The Union forces on Little Round Top were led by Colonel Joshua Lawrence Chamberlain, who was a professor at Bowdoin College in Maine and spoke nine languages. Although he enlisted with no prior military experience, by war's end, Chamberlain had been promoted to brigadier general and was awarded the Medal of Honor after being wounded six times. He later served as governor of Maine.

Round Top Rout

As the Southern troops clamber up Little Round Top, Union soldiers stand up from behind a ledge of rocks and assault the regiment with rifle blasts. When Oates leads an uphill charge toward the enemy, a Union officer cries, "Come on, boys!" Moments later, shouting bluecoats run downhill, bayonets thrust forward, and the shocked Confederates stampede back down Little Round Top, running for their lives.

Germ Warfare

About 620,000 soldiers were killed during the Civil War. Around 206,000 died from wounds, and 416,000 perished from diseases such as typhus, typhoid, dysentery, pneumonia, measles, mumps, malaria, gangrene, and all kinds of surgical infections.

Taking a Hit

As 1,600 Confederates reached Cemetery Ridge on July 2, they were met by hundreds of Minnesota troops, who held off the Confederates until reinforcements arrived. Within five minutes, only 47 Minnesotans were left standing. The rest—82 percent of the regiment—were killed or wounded. That was the highest casualty percentage of any Union regiment in the war.

Hospital Duty

Back at Seminary Ridge, you are ordered to stretcher duty. You help carry a groaning soldier to a tented field hospital. Inside, near a pile of arms and legs, a surgeon stands over a soldier whose leg bone has been shattered by a bullet. An overworked assistant surgeon places a cloth soaked in **chloroform** over the soldier's mouth and nose to render the patient unconscious. The surgeon picks up a small saw and **amputates** the soldier's leg at the knee. The procedure happens quickly, as he slices through muscle and ligaments, and ties off veins and arteries. When the surgery ends, the doctor wipes his hands and the saw on a bloody towel and prepares for the next patient.

field hospital at Gettysburg, Pennsylvania, July 1863

July 3, Morning: A Bold Plan

Early on July 3, the men **grouse** that the South gained little ground yesterday. Covering much of the area today are the bodies of the dead, and men lugging big cameras are photographing the scene.

Minutes later, Lee's lieutenants are called for a council on Seminary Ridge. Lee will bombard the enemy, then attack Cemetery Ridge, while Ewell takes Culp's Hill. But in the morning, part of the plan goes awry: Ewell's forces on Culp's Hill are defeated by a Union assault.

By noon, a lull in the fighting leaves the battlefield so silent you hear birds twittering. It is oddly peaceful given the last two days.

Lee's Plan for Freed Slaves

Lee fought for his native Virginia and the South. He believed slavery was harmful, but he didn't think white and black people could live together equally in the United States. Instead, Lee was in favor of returning enslaved people to Africa to form new, free nations.

Lee vs. Longstreet

You find out that Lee is upset by Ewell's defeat, and Lee asks Longstreet his opinion of the battle plan. Longstreet again tries to convince Lee that the troops should "move around to the right of Meade's army, and maneuver him into attacking us."

Lee disagrees, saying he will send 15,000 men against the Union army at Cemetery Ridge. Longstreet replies, "I think I can safely say there never was a body of 15,000 men who could make that attack successfully." Lee is your hero. What if Lee's wrong?

Photo Finish

More than 3,000 photographers snapped pictures of Civil War battlefields. One of the most famous is Mathew Brady, who helped document Gettysburg's aftermath. Photographers made portraits and took photos of fallen soldiers and destroyed buildings, rather than men in action. They did this because the film they used needed a long exposure time, so any movement would have shown up as a blur.

Day of Destiny

This map shows the positions and movements of the Union and Confederate armies on July 3, 1863. This was the fateful day that changed the course of the Civil War.

4:30 a.m. Union **artillery** bombards the Confederate position near the bottom of Culp's Hill. Soon after, the Union infantry attacks. By 11 a.m., the Confederates will retreat.

9 a.m. The Confederate infantry at Seminary Ridge gets ready to charge. Recently arrived troops led by George Pickett are chosen to take part in the attack, as well as divisions commanded by Isaac Trimble and James Pettigrew.

12 p.m. East of Gettysburg (not visible on the map), mounted soldiers led by J. E. B. Stuart try to get behind Union lines. Union forces, led by George A. Custer, keep the Confederates from gaining ground.

1 p.m. Confederate artillery starts shelling Cemetery Ridge. Many bombs land on the backside of the ridge and do little damage. Union artillery bombards Seminary Ridge, hitting about 900 soldiers.

2:30 p.m. The Union stops its bombardment. This fools the Confederates into thinking it's safe to attack.

3:30 p.m. About 15,000 Confederate troops begin to march toward Cemetery Ridge. They are blasted by Union artillery and infantry. Some get past the Union line at the Angle before being driven off.

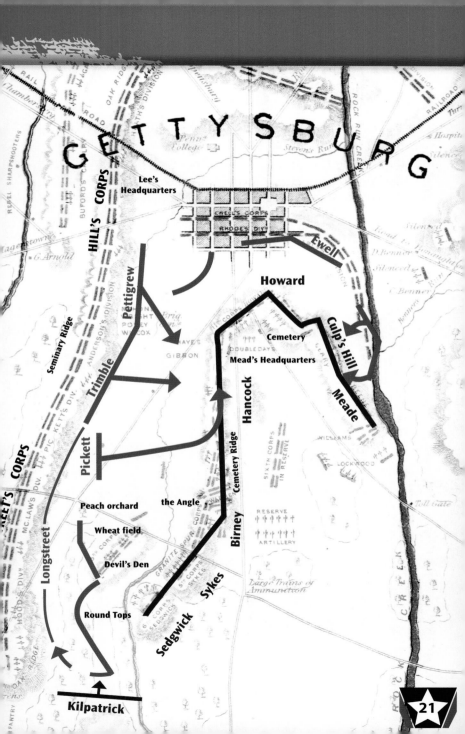

GETTYSBURG

REBEL SHARPSHOOTERS

RAIL ROAD

OAK RIDGE

HILL'S CORPS

Lee's Headquarters

EWELL'S CORPS
RHODE'S DIV.

Ewell

Pettigrew

Howard

Seminary Ridge

Trimble

Cemetery

Mead's Headquarters

Culp's Hill

Pickett

Hancock

Meade

LONGSTREET'S CORPS

Cemetery Ridge

Longstreet

Peach orchard

the Angle

Wheat field

Birney

Devil's Den

SIXTH CORPS IN RESERVE

RESERVE
ARTILLERY

Round Tops

Sykes

Sedgwick

Kilpatrick

21

July 3, Afternoon: A Slaughter

This afternoon, the hot, heavy air and ominous silence leave the army on edge. At 1 p.m., two cannon shots signal the start of the artillery barrage. All at once, hundreds of guns blast away at Cemetery Ridge, sending flames leaping from their muzzles and shells flying through the air like meteors. Soon, a huge haze of gun smoke drifts east, obscuring Cemetery Ridge. When the smoke clears, the artillery crews realize they aimed too high, causing many shells to miss their targets and land on the back side of the ridge.

Break from the Battle

As John E. Dooley's Virginia infantry approached the Yankee guns on Cemetery Ridge, the soldiers stopped near a group of apple trees. Dooley later wrote, ". . . while we are resting here we amuse ourselves by pelting each other with green apples. So frivolous men can be even in the hour of death."

Ready to Rumble

The Union artillery fires back, forcing you to duck as shells burst in the woods around Seminary Ridge. The deadly **salvo** hits many soldiers and makes the ground shake. Around 2:45 p.m., the Union guns go quiet, seemingly out of ammo. The Confederate bombardments stop soon after—it's time to attack. The men line up on the east side of Seminary Ridge, gazing across the three-quarter-mile (1.2 kilometers) open field they must cross. In the distance, behind a long stone wall near the base of Cemetery Ridge, a row of Northern soldiers aims rifles at the Southerners.

Long Shots

The farthest an artillery shell could travel was around two miles (3.2 kilometers). But the guns were not very accurate for targets more than half a mile away.

One of the Confederate generals leading the attack is George E. Pickett, a dashing figure with nearly shoulder-length hair. He shouts, "Charge the enemy, and remember Old Virginia!" As you beat the drum, troops in a line almost a mile long start marching in perfect unison.

When the Confederate troops reach the barren space of the open field, around 75 Union cannons open fire—they weren't out of ammunition after all! **Shrapnel** from a single burst hits as many as 10 soldiers, but the line keeps moving forward, soldiers filling in the gaps as their **comrades** fall to the ground. No one is permitted to return fire, even when Union soldiers fire **volleys** of bullets. Hundreds, and then thousands of soldiers crumple. The Southerners are sitting ducks, but the line moves ahead nonetheless.

Angle of Attack

Endless Union fire hits both ends of the line, forcing Confederates to the middle of Cemetery Ridge. This spot is called the Angle because a stone wall juts out in an L shape here. Union cannons fire until the shells run out. Confederate General Lewis A. Armistead climbs the wall, bellowing, "Who will follow me?" Troops fight hand to hand, tripping over fallen bodies. Soon, soldiers who had crossed the wall were wounded, captured, or dead. The survivors race back to Seminary Ridge.

a portion of Philippoteaux's cyclorama

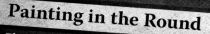

Painting in the Round

The most impressive—or at least the biggest—painting to depict the Civil War is a scene showing Pickett's charge. Painted by French artist Paul Philippoteaux, *The Battle of Gettysburg* is a cyclorama—a canvas arranged in a circle so spectators can get a 360° view of the scene. The painting was restored to its original measurements: 42 feet (13 meters) high and 377 feet (115 meters) around. It is located in the Gettysburg Museum and Visitor Center in Pennsylvania.

Three Bloody Days

The total number of casualties in the three days of the Battle of Gettysburg was higher than all previous American wars combined. The total Confederate dead, wounded, or missing was 28,000—close to 40 percent of those who fought. The Union total was 23,000, or about 25 percent of those who fought.

Picking Up the Pieces

The South has lost the Battle of Gettysburg. A roll call confirms that over 6,500 Southern troops were killed, wounded, or captured in less than an hour today. It's about half the men who took part in the attack. Lee rides by and apologizes to the troops for this bitter defeat and warns them that they need to prepare to defend themselves. He expects Meade to finish off the Confederate army. You're relieved when it becomes clear that Lee is wrong—Meade isn't counterattacking.

Final Resting Place

More than 3,500 Union soldiers are buried at the Gettysburg National Cemetery. The battlefield and national cemetery together form the Gettysburg National Military Park, where close to 1,400 monuments, markers, and memorials commemorate the Battle of Gettysburg.

The Beginning of the End

That evening, word spreads that the army will prepare for its return to Virginia. Lee's army has suffered too many casualties and is far too low on ammunition and supplies to stay in enemy territory. The Southern strategy is being criticized because it allowed the Union to dig into the high ground and ultimately led the South to foolishly attack the Union's center.

The South will fight on, but you wonder if the Battle of Gettysburg will be the turning point in the war. It isn't likely Lee will ever invade the North again, and the Union must now feel better about its chances. The next morning, heavy rains begin to fall over Gettysburg, and everything looks bleak to you and the rest of Lee's army.

On Hallowed Ground

On November 19, 1863, President Abraham Lincoln traveled to Gettysburg, where he dedicated a military cemetery (now the Gettysburg National Cemetery). There he delivered the Gettysburg Address. He wasn't the main speaker of the day, but Lincoln's 272-word speech, assuring that the war would bring the nation "a new birth of freedom," is one of the most important in U.S. history.

Glossary

amputates—cuts off in surgery

artillery—the part of the army that uses large guns that shoot great distances

bayonet—a long knife attached to the front end of a rifle used as a weapon in close combat

chagrin—annoyance; frustration

chloroform—a dangerous liquid sometimes used as an anesthetic during surgery

cohorts—group of soldiers; companions; colleagues

comrades—fellow soldiers

courier—a person who delivers packages and messages

demoralize—to cause someone to lose hope or confidence

enfilade—gunfire from the side of an enemy position instead of straight on

erroneous—incorrect

exhorts—tries to influence or urge someone into action

foraging—searching or grazing for supplies, food, etc.

grouse—complain

haversack—a kind of knapsack worn over the shoulder

infantry—the part of the army that fights on foot

militia—a group of people not part of the armed forces but are trained like soldiers

muskets—long rifles that load from the muzzle, used by infantry soldiers

muzzle—the front end of the barrel of a rifle or revolver

ramrod—a long rod used to push bullets and gunpowder down the barrel of a rifle

ridge—a long, narrow, raised length of land

salvo—the firing of multiple guns at the same time

shrapnel—the small metal fragments of an exploded bomb

skirmish—an unplanned fight during a war

teeming—overflowing

volleys—large numbers of bullets shot at the same time

Index

Check It Out!

Books

Anderson, Tanya. 2013. *Tillie Pierce: Teen Eyewitness to the Battle of Gettysburg*. Twenty-First Century Books.

Bradford, Ned, ed. 2001. *Battles and Leaders of the Civil War*. Gramercy Publishing Company.

Editors of *TIME* Magazine. 2013. *TIME Gettysburg*. Time Inc. Books.

Hunt, Irene. 2002. *Across Five Aprils*. Jam Books.

Johnson, Jennifer. 2009. *Gettysburg: The Bloodiest Battle of the Civil War*. Scholastic Inc.

Ward, Geoffrey C. 1990. *The Civil War: An Illustrated History*. Alfred A. Knopf, Inc.

Weber, Jennifer L. 2010. *Summer's Bloodiest Days: The Battle of Gettysburg as Told from All Sides*. National Geographic Children's Books.

Video

History Channel. *American Civil War History*.

Websites

Civil War Trust. *Gettysburg*. http://www.civilwar.org /battlefields/gettysburg.html.

National Park Service. *Gettysburg*. http://www.nps.gov /gett/index.htm.

Try It!

The Battle of Gettysburg was one of the most important battles of the Civil War and is often referred to as the "turning point" in the war. Imagine you are the drummer for a different battle in the Civil War. Your sole responsibility, aside from directing and leading the army with your drum, is to log all that is taking place on the battlefield. Before beating your drum, you have some work to do:

- Research other battles of the Civil War. Make sure to investigate important figures, locations, and events from each battle.

- Decide which battle you want to write about. Are you in support of the North or the South?

- Start writing. Format your entries as a journal (date, salutation, closing, etc.). In your entries, make sure to include historical information. If the battle spans a few days, write one journal entry for every day or every other day. Be creative in your descriptions. Describe your feelings about how the battle is playing out. Don't forget to discuss your role as a drummer.

- Look over your entries and give them to a friend to suggest edits.

- Rewrite your journal entries on vintage paper and bind them together with twine.

- Read your favorite entry to the class.

About the Author

Born and raised in Brooklyn, New York, Curtis Slepian received a master's degree in English literature from the University of Michigan. He has worked as an editor at the puzzle magazine *Games*, the kids' science magazine *Contact Kids*, and at *TIME FOR KIDS Learning Ventures*. Among the books he has written are *Animal Adventures 3D*, *Big Book of How*, *TIME FOR KIDS United States Atlas*, and *That's Incredible*. He currently lives in New York City, where he enjoys reading books about history, especially those on the Civil War.